CHOPPERS

MIKE SEATE

photography by MICHAEL LICHTER

CRESTLINE

This edition published in 2004 by Crestline, an imprint of MBI Publishing Company, Galtier Plaza, Suite 200, 380 Jackson Street, St. Paul, MN 55101-3885 USA

First published in 2004 by MBI Publishing Company.

© Michael Lichter and Mike Seate, 2004

Crestline books are also available at discounts in bulk quantity for industrial or sales-promotional use. For details, please contact: Special Sales Manager at MBI Publishing Company, Galtier Plaza, Suite 200, 380 Jackson Street, St. Paul, MN 55101-3885 USA.

For a free catalog, call 1-800-826-6600, or visit our website at www.motorbooks.com.

ISBN 0-7603-2124-8

Printed in China

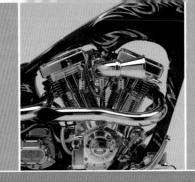

CONTENTS

SECTION 2

YOUNG GUNS 82

Photographer's Notes

BY MICHAEL LICHTER

The photographs in this book were taken over many years and many miles. The pavement has blurred beneath me. Cameras, backgrounds, and the style of photography has changed since I started riding and photographing this subject in the 1970s, just as the style of custom bikes and the bike builders themselves have changed.

Now, in this new millennium, custom bike builders are looking back to an earlier time, to the choppers of the 1960s, for inspiration. Choppers are the rage, fueled by the many fires repeatedly aired on cable television. Those of us who remember the phenomenon the first time around are feeling a bit nostalgic for those wild times. Kids seeing it now ache for that first chopper ride, just the way we did when the film *Easy Rider* was released in 1969.

Once again, choppers influenced by the trends of the 1960s are being built in backyard garages and custom motorcycle shops of all sizes. People are trying their hand at fabricating for the first time. Brimming with excitement and energy, young builders are bringing new ideas to the table and finding new twists on old looks. They are cutting, grinding, and welding in places that never would have seen sparks before. If the drivetrain has always been on the left, they will put it on the right.

FROM LEFT: Unknown, James Simonelli, Roger Bourget, Brett Smith, Bill Rucker, Unknown, Pat Matter, Arlen Ness. Daytona Beach, 2003.

They will enlarge the brake rotor to the size of the rim or hide it altogether within the guts of the motorcycle. They will use technology to its fullest or, just as easily, they will turn around and ignore it, going back to jockey shifts, springer front ends, drum brakes, and rigid frames. Questioning the established order, anything goes in the exploration that will eventually lead to a style these new builders will call their own. The only rules are "There are no rules."

There is a big age difference between the legends we highlight in this book, builders who have been plying their craft for more than forty years, and the younger metal benders who were born after I took my first Shovelhead road trip from California to Colorado in 1977. Young and old alike, however, share a common love of motorcycles and a need to put their personal signatures on each of their creations. You can ask both the legends and the new bloods what first attracted them to bikes and you will probably hear similar responses: that they saw a movie, had a friend who rode, knew of some cool bikes in their hometown, or they raced as kids. Few went to technical trade schools, business plans were uncommon, and goals were very short term. Whatever the hook that brought them into biking, it seems universal that it struck a deep passionate chord within. It was love at first sight.

Billy Lane runs into Paul Yaffe at Daytona, 2004.

This common passion led many of these bike builders to choose motorcycle fabrication as a way of life. Not looking for a ride to fame and fortune (although some are experiencing this now) they felt lucky to be able to support themselves doing something they truly enjoyed. Moving from backyard garages to commercial spaces, their businesses grew—many hired helpers, then sales staff. Incredible bikes were being built for themselves and customers.

The same passion continues to drive the motorcycle business today and the chopper craze is heating it up more, like a hit of nitrous, accelerating activity and interest. There have been shops with names like Frisco Choppers for a long time (I bought my Shovelhead there in the 1970s), but once Jesse James began to get so much attention for his West Coast Choppers, the chopper industry absolutely exploded.

Tom Langton, Joey Perse, and Roger Goldammer at the Biker's Ball, Daytona, 2004.

Now you have Orange County Choppers, New York City Choppers, East Coast Choppers, No Coast Choppers, and probably a hundred others with similar names. You also have the hit television show *American Choppers*, which consumes non-riders and riders alike. Everyone is talking choppers. It's sizzling to the point that thousands of customs are rolling out of factories each year from companies such as American Ironhorse, Big Dog, Swift, and Vengeance. They mostly produce choppers with model names like "Texas Chopper," "Bar Chopper," or simply "Chopper." Get the picture? Choppers are riding the crest of this custom motorcycling tidal wave.

You would imagine that "Chopper" would have a very clear and precise definition, but more and more it is used interchangeably with the word "custom" as it refers to a motorcycle, especially with the general public. The term has entered the lexicon. It is still used by traditionalists to describe a bike that was chopped (or cut) at its neck so the front end could be raked (or extended) out, often 20 inches or more. There are many other defining traits, but as long as builders keep using the "No Rules" policy, choppers will be even harder to pigeon hole.

Paul Cox and Indian Larry, flying through Tomoka State Park, 2004.

Billy Lane, Eddie Trotta, Unknown, Tom Langton, and
Kendall Johnson, debuting Camel bikes, Daytona, 2003.

Paul Cox, Chica, Unknown, Johnny Vasko, and Indian
Larry, Daytona Beach, 2004.

While my focus is photography rather than customizing bikes, the same experiences drew me to motorcycles. I saw *Easy Rider* when it came out on the big screen, but it wasn't until a friend let me ride his long chopped 1947 Harley-Davidson Knucklehead that I heard the music. Six months later, I was riding back to Colorado from San Francisco on my own chopped Shovelhead, photographing the bike and landscape throughout the trip. I loved bikes, loved riding, and loved taking photos but never thought I would or could have a life that revolved around this. Like many of the builders, I have never written a business plan, and I never will.

Because this section is called "Photographer's Notes," some of you may be interested in this photographer's notes regarding photography. The changes in photography I referred to in my opening paragraph have been enormous. Personally, I was shooting for myself through most of the 1970s, so I shot exactly how I wanted to: with one 35mm camera mounted with a 35mm lens and loaded with black-and-white film. By the early 1980s, I was on assignment for *Easyriders* and began shooting color slide film in addition to the black and white. There were multiple camera bodies and a barrage of lenses. By 1982, bike features entered my repertoire. I began shooting in my own studio (the same studio I still shoot in) with medium format 6x6cm Hasselblad cameras using quartz lights at first and then studio strobes. In the late 1980s, I started using slightly larger Mamiya cameras with their 6x7cm image, and solid painted backgrounds gave way to large hand-painted canvases. By 1998, the Mamiya gave way to big Fuji 6x8cm cameras and the painted muslins were put away as I returned to painting the studio and shooting bike features on plain backgrounds.

A question that often comes up is why I shoot most of my bike features in the studio on plain backgrounds. For me, the *bike* is the art. I am just a facilitator, translating the three-dimensional piece to two dimensions and bringing it to the public eye. By controlling the light and the background, the focus stays on the bike. I have always felt chrome looks better with smooth neutral reflections that help shape the metal rather than strong colored reflections, green grass, or asphalt. As for camera angles, I spend way to much time on my knees and laying on my stomach, but to look up at a bike makes it seem even more monumental. It puts a little twist on what is normally seen from eye level and hopefully creates more interest for the viewer. It is about power and grace, muscle and style.

I brought the most significant photographic change upon myself in 2000 when I began shooting digital. A loyal Kodak film user for over thirty years, my film purchases began to decline slowly and

Matt Burris and Kim Suter, Biker Ball, Daytona, 2004.

steadily until by 2003 they hit zero. In the studio, I use a Leaf Scitex digital camera system with a large liquid-cooled chip in the back and Nikon lenses up front. I could put the digital back on any of my medium-format camera bodies or larger 4x5 cameras but choose to run it with an integrated live video system. There isn't even a viewfinder to look through on this beast but it sure does scream! Everything is done on the computer, composing, adjusting, capturing, processing, and archiving. In the field, I shoot with two Nikon D1x's. To process the large quantity of raw images I generate, I have a number of Apple Macintosh computers. What may be more interesting than this technical laundry list is just imagining packing a Harley for a road trip with two of these sophisticated Nikon digital cameras, two titanium Macintosh laptop computers, back-up hard drives, more than five spare lenses, strobes, camera supports, bags, and plenty of miscellaneous gear. Clothing and toiletries get stuffed wherever they fit. It really is quite an achievement!

I have come a long way since just shooting images for myself. In addition to shooting the bikes, I shoot many motorcycle events for *Easyriders*, brochures and catalogues for the manufacturers, and have returned to exhibiting work from my archive in galleries and museums. I couldn't do it all without help. I took on my first full-time assistant in the mid-1980s and have had at least one assistant on my staff ever since. Steve Temple has been with me since 1999 and he does such an incredible job keeping all this digital equipment running—and me shooting—that I have affectionately dubbed him the "Wizard." He deserves a lot of credit.

Billy Lane riding with Mondo Porras, 2004.

I would also like to thank the many builders who have allowed me to include their photographs in this book. I have known them for years (several for more than twenty) and consider many my personal friends. They have been most gracious in giving me the time I needed to do their bikes justice. While I am mentioning them last, first in my heart is my wife Catherine and children Sean and Kiera, who have been wonderful at allowing me to indulge in this bizarre pastime and business for as long as they can remember.

Special thanks go to my uncle Jules for taking me into the darkroom in 1960, to Richie Schiff's mom, Charlotte, for getting us into the film *Easy Rider* even though we weren't 16 yet, and to Grosvenor for letting me ride that Knucklehead of his and planting the seed.

If you are interested in reading more about my work and seeing more imagery, you can visit my website at www.lichterphoto.com.

—Michael Lichter

LEGENDS

It takes a good 10 years to become an overnight sensation according to the old show-business cliché, but that cliché could easily apply to chopper builders as well as entertainers. Most of the legendary builders whose names are seen in lights at Daytona, Sturgis, Laughlin, and other international motorcycle functions have busted their knuckles for decades, working long weekends and enduring sleepless nights to achieve acclaim in the custom motorcycle world.

Most of these master craftsmen are surprisingly humble in person; their years of toil and reward seem to have rendered them a shade more human than many of their younger, brasher counterparts who, in recent years, have found the road to chopper-building success far easier than it was for the legends. This is at least in part because the hard work of the legends paved their way.

It's easy to forget in today's world of six-figure designer choppers, celebrity chopper riders, and a thriving custom-motorcycle scene that the legendary builders began their careers not only in obscurity, but in a field where their creations were largely shunned by the mainstream motorcycle community. There weren't any full-color gatefolds of choppers gracing the pages of mainstream cycle magazines like *Cycle World* a few decades ago. If you saw a custom motorcycle on TV, it was either due to news coverage of a bike club getting busted by the law, or you were watching an old Peter Fonda flick on the late, late show. It wasn't uncommon for chopper builders to have their shops investigated by the law or shaken down by the local cops just because of the way their employees dressed or the type of motorcycle they rode for daily transportation.

During the 1980s and early 1990s, choppers were just about the least-fashionable style of motorcycle a rider could imagine. Custom Harleys of the period were massively wide, nostalgia-heavy fatbikes painted in pastel colors and adorned with cornball regalia like fringed leather saddlebags, buckhorn handlebars, and two-tone cowhide seat covers. They looked like rolling Good Humor trucks or novelty machines ridden by Shriners on parade.

To say the legends of the industry deserve the props currently being heaped on them by the press and electronic media is putting it mildly; there are no overnight sensations here. The legendary chopper builders are finally reaping the rewards of their blood, sweat, toil, and talent.

Chapter 1

Arlin Fatland

ROCKY MOUNTAIN COOL

Colorado's Arlin Fatland has what you might call a wicked sense of humor. As proprietor of Denver's 2 Wheeler's Motorcycle Shop, Fatland once offered his female customers "free installation" on underwear orders.

His choppers have always revealed a playful, almost childlike sense of fun. He once designed an entire custom Harley-Davidson Softail to match a set of snakeskin cowboy boots he'd purchased, and it's not unusual to see wacky details like the bulging eyes from the old Moon auto parts ad painted on the tanks and fenders of one of Fatland's choppers.

Though the accessory department at 2 Wheelers has enough stock to assemble a dozen bikes right off the shelves, Fatland is a stickler for one-off fabrication and handmade detailing to really set his bikes apart from the crowd. A skilled bodyman as well as a sheetmetal manipulator, Fatland seldom leaves fenders and tanks in their stock form; most are stretched, widened, molded, or altered in some way before they're bolted onto a finished motorcycle. A Fatland exhaust system is often constructed to mimic the flex-tube piping on old Harley-Davidson Flatheads of the 1940s, while whitewall tires, Maltese cross mirrors, magneto ignitions with kick-starters, and other style icons that wouldn't look out of place on movie-biker Erik Von Zipper's bike are common.

A fan of custom choppers and bobbers from the 1950s, Fatland's machines are frequently painted with elaborate two-tone scallops or checkered flag motifs like those found on early drag bikes. "Some of the classic stuff just never goes out of style, no matter what everybody else is building at the time. I remember the bikes and cars I saw when I was a boy and I always tend to come back to that," he said.

Frame: **Rigid**

Engine: **Evolution-type**

Date Photographed: **2001**

Frame: **Rigid**

Engine: **Panhead**

Date Photographed: **1992**

Frame: **Rigid**

Engine: **Knucklehead**

Date Photographed: **1995**

Chapter 2

Don Hotop

CORN-FED CUSTOMS

Don Hotop started building choppers as a result of a game of 8-ball back in 1969. He won an old 1939 Harley-Davidson Flathead 45-cubic-incher in a pool-hall bet and decided to reinvent the machine. He built it to resemble the choppers he'd seen local motorcycle clubs riding.

He discovered he had a talent for building choppers. For a while the Fort Meade, Iowa, resident worked day shifts at a local Chevron Oil chemical plant and customized Harleys for local bikers by night. A lay-off in 1977 prompted him to take up chopper building full time.

Hotop said, "I've always just enjoyed working on choppers and after building custom Harleys in my garage, I just kept at it until I got better and better and became a fool for it."

Though Hotop is refreshingly modest, he's no fool when it comes to the chopper trade: a self-taught bodyman and mechanic, his shop, Don's Speed and Custom, now offers Midwestern riders everything from ground-up custom choppers to performance tuning, sheetmetal parts, and custom paint. He was commissioned to design a one-off custom machine for Victory motorcycles in 2001, and many of Hotop's sublime details found their way onto late-model V92C Victory cruisers.

These days Don's churns out about a half-dozen complete project motorcycles each year, bikes the builder says are infused with a "practical, no-nonsense approach to choppers. My machines are built with an emphasis on fine finishes, reasonable rakes, and engines that are powerful, but not so big they're breaking down all the time. I build dependable choppers and try and talk customers out of anything too wild. I'd rather have people calling me to say they just had a great ride, not that they broke down somewhere."

For all the runaway mainstream popularity of choppers, Hotop says his customers haven't changed much over the past three decades. Serious chopper riders will come in wanting a machine that will "add a little outlaw to their lives," while the riders inspired by popular television series like American Chopper tend to favor stock Harley-Davidsons with lots of bolt-on parts.

"Those TV shows got a lot of people buying Harleys that never would have even done it had the TV thing not gone on," Hotop said. "But I don't think most of them want anything besides an autograph from one of the stars or a T-shirt. Chopper riders still tend to be real committed guys. Those are my customers."

Frame: **Softail-type**

Engine: **Evolution-type**

Date Photographed: **1995**

Frame: **Rigid**

Engine: **Evolution-type**

Date Photographed: **1995**

Chapter 3
Pat Kennedy
THE COWBOY WAY

In an era when chopper builders can become overnight reality-TV stars, Pat Kennedy of Tombstone, Arizona, is what you might call seriously old school. Kennedy started building choppers as a teenager while wrenching in a small family garage operated by his two chopper-loving older brothers. Rumor has it he left his home in Oceanside, California, for the relative freedom and austerity of Arizona after the helmet law went into effect in California.

Once settled in the dusty, desert hamlet of just 1,300 residents, Kennedy and his wife, Brook, got busy building choppers that incorporate their unpretentious, hard-edged vision of what custom motorcycles should be. Veteran chopper fans say you can spot a Pat Kennedy chopper from across the desert floor; the front ends tend to be longer than an Arizona heat wave, the chassis are decked out with laid-back rake dimensions of 40 degrees or more, and the stretched gas tanks are covered with psychedelic airbrushed murals courtesy of Kennedy's in-house painter, Darrell Pinney.

Self-sufficient and fiercely independent, Kennedy seems content to portray the grizzled outlaw even as many of his contemporaries have adopted a softer, more media-friendly image. His workshop is surrounded by 10-foot-tall fencing, and he's seldom seen without a bandana and blacked-out shades.

But behind the sometimes-intimidating facade is an expert craftsman who is as proud of his creations as any renaissance artist. Kennedy, for example, has never been the type to settle for bolting on aftermarket parts from outside sources. In the past decade, his already impressive line of home-built custom chopper parts has expanded to include items like internal throttle assemblies, adjustable rake trees clamps that allow chopper builders to add up to 15 degrees of additional rake, and painstakingly assembled chromed wire wheels, with 120, 160, or even a dizzying 240 spokes.

One of the first builders to utilize stainless steel for custom motorcycle parts, he's since perfected several exhaust systems and fuel tanks from the durable material. The level of mechanical perfection Kennedy offers customers is partly the result of the Kennedy clan working together as a close-knit team. Brook, herself a chopper rider, laces the wheels, upholsters and designs the seats, and runs the shop office, while Pat designs the look and style of each of the half-dozen choppers that leave the shop each year.

Reflecting the changing nature (and age) of the average chopper rider, Pat's bikes are now split evenly between softail-type frames and rigid-frame rides. Though some of Kennedy's creations may include luxury features like rear suspensions, he still prefers that his bikes be long on style and attitude—just like the man who created them.

Frame: **Softail-type**

Engine: **Evolution-type**

Date Photographed: **1995**

Frame: **Softail-type**

Engine: **Evolution-type**

Date Photographed: **1994**

Frame: **Softail-type**

Engine: **Evolution-type**

Date Photographed: **1997**

Chapter 4
Fred Kodlin
EURO CHOPPERS WITH AN EDGE

Chopper builder Fred Kodlin builds bikes that embody the pride in craftsmanship and unparalleled quality that characterizes machinery from his native Germany. The Borken-based Kodlin vowed to build choppers infused with the same excellence that makes BMW cars and Fokker aircraft class leaders. In the past 24 years, Kodlin has more than surpassed his self-imposed goals of excellence, taking chopper building to new technological and design levels.

Nothing about Kodlin's motorcycles is what you might call traditional—his choppers owe as much to the cutting-edge technology of modern racing bikes as they do to the choppers of old. A Kodlin chopper may be built around a monoshock chassis and covered in a suit of elaborate, hand-sculpted fiberglass bodywork. The lines of his creations flow seamlessly from the one-piece gas tanks to voluptuous, futuristic rear fenders. Kodlin usually uses inverted road racing–style forks.

He often names his techno-pop motorcycles after popular science fiction and adventure films. Kodlin's show-winning chopper "The World Is Not Enough" blew minds and collected trophies from Bohn to Daytona thanks to details that included square-milled telescopic front fork and handlebars, box-shaped exhaust pipes, riveted billet aluminum wheels, and a gas tank that seemed to arch organically across the frame backbone.

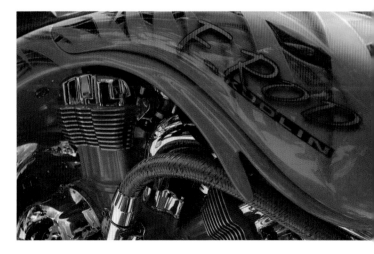

Kodlin, who was the first major chopper builder to approach a project based on Harley-Davidson's water-cooled VSRC V-Rod, has used his innovative ideas to break with the past in ways that shock many chopper purists. But by following his own otherworldly vision, Kodlin has won himself a strong following, along with a worldwide marketing and distribution deal with Custom Chrome Incorporated's European branch. As a result, Kodlin has helped propel European chopper building into a new century with ideas that can startle, surprise, and capture the imagination of all who see them.

Frame: **Softail-type**

Engine: **Twin cam**

Date Photographed: **2001**

Frame: **Softail-type**

Engine: **Twin cam**

Date Photographed: **2001**

Chapter 5

Indian Larry Desmedt

BIG APPLE ATTITUDE

Whether he's riding one of his rigid-framed choppers through a wall of fire on "*Late Night with David Letterman*" or blasting through New York City's urban landscape standing on his seat, Indian Larry (a.k.a. Larry Desmedt) is a chopper legend possessed by a world-class passion.

Growing up in New York's gritty Lower East Side, Larry was bitten by the custom motorcycle bug during the original chopper explosion of the late 1960s. Today, his sought-after motorcycles still embody the elements that made classic choppers into worldwide style icons. You'd be hard-pressed to find a piece of expensive billet aluminum anywhere on one of Larry's creations, and the engines in his rigid sleds tend to boast relatively modest displacements of 80 cubic inches or less.

"Those crazy, 120-inch stroker motors aren't what true choppers are supposed to be about," Larry opined. "To me, a chopper is lightweight, stripped down, and simple. It shouldn't carry anything that doesn't help it go faster or anything that adds weight."

That purist's approach to custom motorcycles is all over Larry's Brooklyn, New York shop, where customers encounter a starkly industrial setting, a hard-working, no-bullshit staff, and hardtail choppers that could have revved across the screen in a Roger Corman movie, circa 1966. Larry is one of the few chopper builders who still adorns his machines with wild, hand-welded sissy bars and bold metalflake paint jobs inspired by famous hot rod cars and visionary fabricators like Ed "Big Daddy" Roth. In an age when many choppers are outfitted with sophisticated suspension systems and multipiston stoppers, an Indian Larry chopper typically rolls on a rigid chassis with a 21-inch front wheel with no brake and no fender for rain protection.

"Choppers," Larry explains in his thick NYC accent, "were like the sportbikes of their day. They broke all the rules and you were likely to see them being ridden hard by some young guy who didn't give a damn what anybody else thought. Guys rode them into the ground and kept their machines simple so they could do their own repairs. That's the way they should always be."

Frame: **Rigid**

Engine: **Shovelhead-Panhead Special Construction**

Date Photographed: **2003**

Frame: **Rigid**

Engine: **Panhead**

Date Photographed: **1998**

Chapter 6
Arlen Ness
THE BAY AREA'S CUSTOM GURU

Nearly 40 years have passed since Arlen Ness of Oakland, California, first took a spray gun and welding torch to a Harley-Davidson motorcycle. In those years, choppers have been the height of fashion, passed out of vogue, and re-emerged once again as the hottest movement in motorcycles. Through it all, the affable and soft-spoken Ness has paused for nary a moment in his quest to redefine the custom motorcycle in his own image.

Despite his lofty position as the world's most respected custom motorcycle builder, Ness actually got a late start in the chopper game. As a young newlywed, his wife wasn't exactly enthused about him riding a motorcycle, so Ness sublimated his two-wheeled passion into customizing choppers for friends in and around the biking hotbed of California's Bay Area. Ness didn't have his own chopper until the age of 27. He paid for that first chopper with earnings from his career as a professional bowler.

After working for a time as a carpenter and long-distance trucker in the mid-1960s, Ness began receiving a deluge of requests for his handmade custom chopper parts. Riders who'd seen him blast by on his custom-painted Knucklehead chopper phoned in pleading for Ness to point an airbrush at their rides too. In time, he opened a small storefront workshop where the first custom Ness parts and entire motorcycles bearing the Arlen Ness signature were created.

Today Ness is best known for complex and visually engaging concept bikes, like his Ness-Tique custom that incorporated design elements from a 1957 Chevy, but when he started his business he focused on the basics. He produced classic chopper accessories like curlicue ram's-horn handlebars, hexagonal gas tanks, and radically raked frames. Contrary to perception, he was never a proponent of the massively extended front ends that characterized California's stretch-chopper movement. "Long front ends always looked kind of dangerous to me, so I lowered my bikes all around, making them like a drag bike," he said. In time, the low-riding, relatively stubby custom choppers Ness perfected became known as "diggers," bikes renowned for their beautifully detailed finishes and revered for their predictable handling.

Even with the success of his aftermarket parts line and custom bikes, the Ness sense of creativity has seldom remained static for long. His current endeavors include a line of high-tech road-racing leathers and a steady output of some 60 ground-up custom motorcycles each year—not a bad output for a hard-riding man of 65.

Frame: **Rigid**

Engine: **Knucklehead**

Date Photographed: **1994**

Frame: **Rigid**

Engine: **Sportster**

Date Photographed: **1994**

Frame: **Rigid**

Engine: **Evolution-type**

Date Photographed: **1999**

Frame: **Rigid**

Engine: **Sportster**

Date Photographed: **1994**

Chapter 7

Donnie Smith

MIDWEST MOTORS

While it's not uncommon to hear choppers described as radical, wicked, and extreme, Minnesota's Donnie Smith wants to create more than a sculpture when he puts torch to metal. He wants to build motorcycles. He wants his customers to enjoy riding his choppers, whether from their homes to their corner taverns or from coast to coast.

Smith, a lanky, cheerful 62-year-old, started riding and chopping motorcycles in the 1970s, at a time when the custom parts aftermarket was in its infancy and mainly outlaws rode choppers. A self-taught welder and mechanic, Smith found himself and his movie-fed love of choppers in the right place at the right time. He got into the business of chopper building in much the same way many other well-known builders did; some of the small modifications he'd performed on friends' bikes became sought after by other riders. Soon Smith's hobby turned into a burgeoning aftermarket career with the 1970s aftermarket powerhouse Smith Brothers & Fetrow.

Though Smith occasionally builds choppers with several inches of stretch in the frame backbones and extended girder forks, his emphasis on function has resulted in machines with relatively short forks, stable rake dimensions, and big-inch motors from the likes of S&S. Not one to shy away from recent advances in braking and driveline technology, Smith uses multipiston billet aluminum braking systems from Performance Machine and G.M.A. A Donnie Smith chopper will stop as quickly as it accelerates. However, Smith is steadfastly traditional when it comes to designing a chassis for one of the 12 choppers he builds each year. He uses no heavy chrome moly steel, preferring lightweight cold-rolled steel for his chassis parts.

In recent years Smith, who has a reputation for being one of the nicest guys in custom bikes, has staged an annual invitational custom bike show in Saint Paul, Minnesota, offering up-and-coming chopper visionaries the chance to display their wares to a broad audience. And Smith's good karma seems to keep returning his way: he was recently chosen alongside chopper masters Dave Perewitz and Arlen Ness to design a limited-edition electric guitar for the Gibson Guitar Corporation. Meanwhile, Viper Motorcycles has enlisted Smith to create a series of custom-made, showroom-ready, mass-produced customs utilizing his unique designs, making his machines available to an even-larger audience.

Frame: **Softail-type**

Engine: **Evolution-type**

Date Photographed: **2000**

Frame: **Softail-type**

Engine: **Evolution-type**

Date Photographed: **2002**

Frame: **Softail-type**

Engine: **Panhead-type**

Date Photographed: **1997**

Chapter 8

Eddie Trotta

LUST FOR LIFE

Any discussion of the career and life of Fort Lauderdale's Eddie Trotta should be accompanied by a few riffs from Iggy Pop's hedonist anthem "Lust for Life." Trotta's rise to the top of the chopper game came after the New Haven, Connecticut, native had spent decades racing thoroughbred horses, studying music, and later competing in—and winning—the prestigious Baccardi Cup speedboat race. In his spare time he managed to build a business empire.

But while Trotta was busy globetrotting and living the high life, he actually maintained his teenage love of building and designing custom choppers, a skill he'd learned while wrenching at a local custom bike shop. So by 2001 when Trotta emerged on the international chopper stage with an over-the-top stretch chopper he'd been commissioned to design for the Camel Roadhouse bike showcase, more than a few of his contemporaries wondered where this new jack got all the skills.

Truth is, Trotta never stopped brainstorming about choppers during the 30-year interval between his early bike-building apprenticeship and the launch of Thunder Cycle Designs in 1991. In a brief amount of time, he was able to produce an extensive line of high-end choppers and parts, gaining widespread industry accolades for the low-slung frames and swooping, liquid bodywork that charac-terized Trotta's fresh take on chopper styling. He was among the first proponents of the single-sided swingarm for choppers, a design that is now popular with builders the world over, while his inverted front forks provide unheard-of levels of roadway stability for chopped motorcycles. Long, low, and built from some of the thickest frame tubing and beefiest forks on the market, Trotta's machines capture their builder's lust for life in spades.

Frame: **Softail-type**

Engine: **Evolution-type**

Date Photographed: **1998**

Frame: **Rigid**

Engine: **Evolution-type**

Date Photographed: **2001**

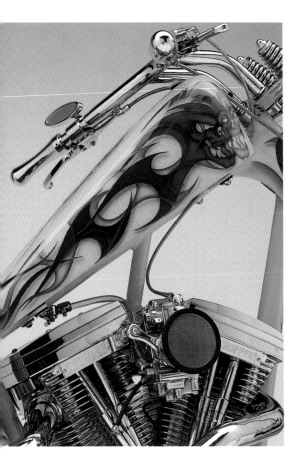

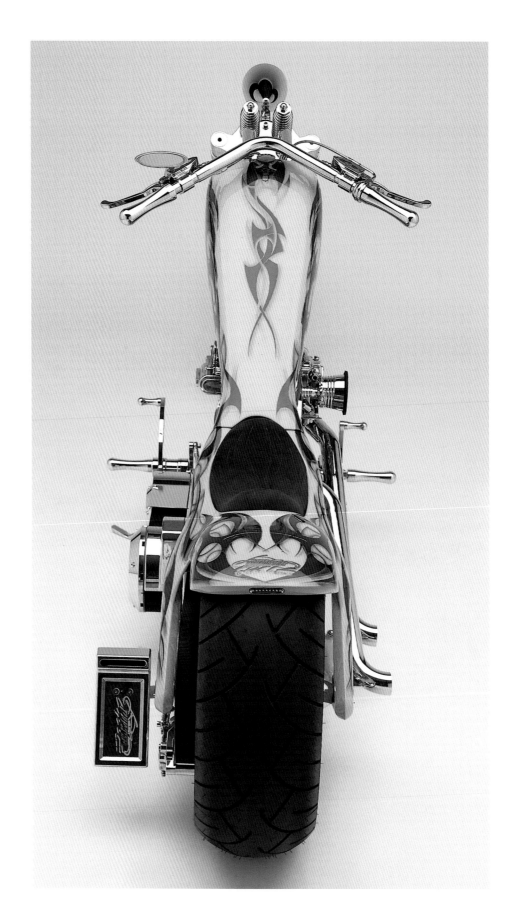

Frame: **Softail-type**

Engine: **Evolution-type**

Date Photographed: **2003**

YOUNG GUNS

Talk with most any of today's notable custom motorcycle builders and they'll speak passionately of schedules full of 17-hour days, tired nights spent falling asleep at the drawing boards, and more publicity tours and autograph sessions than a top-selling rock star sees in a year.

Most of the hot builders barely have time to ride their choppers. During the riding season they face a flurry of national custom motorcycle shows or TV appearances, each of which places almost surreal demands on their individual work forces, artistic skills, and patience. When you've got a fender that doesn't line up with your hand-poured seat pan, a chromer who seems to have disappeared with your rocker box covers two days before a national show, and a 113-cubic-inch stroker engine that won't fire with a film crew's cameras rolling, riding a motorcycle is about the last thing on a young builder's mind.

It takes more than just a smart hand with an airbrush and talent with an arc welder to get your machines noticed in today's highly competitive, big-money chopper game. Building bikes that run as hard as they look, bikes that captivate the public's imagination even when there's some wiseacre with an even better idea waiting just around the bend, isn't easy. Maybe it shouldn't be. The following builders have all met those challenges and more and managed to come out on top. Props to 'em.

Chapter 9
Tank Ewsichek
RIDDEN HARD, PUT AWAY SATISFIED

Building the perfect, timeless chopper is no stretch for Ohio's Tank Ewsichek. He remembers vividly a little hole-in-the-wall chopper shop in his family's Garfield Heights neighborhood, a place where bikers would ride through the shop's doors on bone-stock Harley-Davidson Superglides and Electra Glides in the early 1970s and roll out a few weeks later on radically customized choppers.

"I can still remember those bikes today," he says wistfully, "and to me, the sky-high apehangers, the long forks, and the wild paint are still what makes a chopper a chopper." The neighborhood biker hangout left such an impression on Tank that by the age of 13 he'd grown bored with trying to adapt discarded parts from the local chopper shop's garbage pile to his bicycles and started customizing motorcycles himself. First came a Harley-Davidson Sprint street-and-trail bike that was soon followed by an old XLCH Sportster that was purchased used for $2,100. Today, Tank says not much has changed when it comes to building and riding choppers, though the customers, he laughs, "tend to cry a lot more than they used to when they see the bills."

Tank admits it's not cheap to order a hand-built chopper from his shop, Tuff Cycles, located in Aurora, Ohio. He puts in some serious man-hours in a workshop that's conveniently located just 15 feet or so from his family home. Despite the efforts of a full-time crew of four, Tank's days are hectic, backbreaking affairs; on the day we called on him, for example, he'd worked until 11 p.m. the previous night. The following workday began at sunrise and he fully expected another long night spent finishing one of his sinewy, stripped-down customs.

Working this hard is nothing new, he says. As a teen, Tank spent his days learning the sheetmetal-shaping and custom-painting trade in his father's auto repair shop and spent his nights building custom Harleys for local riders. Since then, his motorcycles, known for their classic, 1960s styling and extraordinary paintwork, have been featured in museum shows and biker gatherings across the United States and Europe, but Tank, ever modest, remains a hometown boy unimpressed with the glitz and glamour of the big-money chopper set.

"Yeah, they showed some of my bikes in London and Stockholm, but those are places I never would have gone on my own. There's some talented guys building choppers over there, but I'd rather just ride one of my own bikes and put in a long day at the shop," he said.

Frame: **Rigid**

Engine: **Evolution-type**

Date Photographed: **1997**

Frame: **Rigid**

Engine: **Evolution-type**

Date Photographed: **1999**

Frame: **Softail-type**

Engine: **Evolution-type**

Date Photographed: **2000**

Chapter 10
Rick Fairless
NO FEAR OF SUCCESS

Epitomizing the Texas ethos of playing big in life, fun, and work is Dallas native Rick Fairless. He started his career in bikes as a backyard customizer, a trade he learned while engaged in a winning career as a paint salesman. His familiarity with finishes served Fairless well when, in 1996, he opened up Stroker's Dallas, a massive custom motorcycle shop, restaurant, and accessories retail outlet.

Like most adventures in his life, Fairless wasn't satisfied with just running a successful dealership specializing in aftermarket Big Twins from Big Dog and American Ironhorse. In time, his family was working beside him in the shop, a popular rider's destination, doing everything from organizing charity rides to cooking burgers and staging entertainment for visitors. Fairless eventually added his own custom creations to the shop's already busy showroom floor, machines that proved to be a hit with national celebrities, members of Texas' burgeoning oil-money set, and professional athletes. Fairless now employs two full-time builders and a trio of parts fabricators.

A Fairless custom follows no distinct historical periods or creative limits; his bikes are just as likely to be reworked, late-model Harley-Davidson Road Kings—albeit Road Kings with fire-breathing, 95-cubic-inch motors, chrome Carriage Works rims, and Baker six-speed trannies—as they are to be mind-bending longbikes. An example of the latter style is his radically raked Psychedelic Chopper, adorned with airbrushed portraits of 1960s icons from Frank Zappa to John and Yoko to Charles Manson.

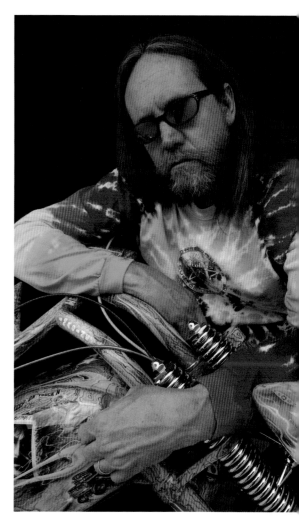

"The Psychedelic bike came about because I still love the 1960s and the music from those days, so I started designing it to represent all the stuff I'm interested in," said Fairless.

Some of his other choppers have required more divine—and sometimes playful—inspiration. Take the Six Pack Chopper, which resembles a pair of rolling beer cans linked together with pool cues. That bike came about "after downing a few beers with some friends," Fairless said. Sometimes his customers provide his inspiration. His flash-covered Tattoo Chopper resembles the owner's heavily inked clientele.

"I get my inspiration for these bikes from just about anywhere because I'm good at visualizing a bike before it's built," Fairless said. "My guys at the shop all chime in with ideas and they all donate something to the finished product. That way, we're all proud of what comes out."

With so many ideas manifesting themselves in metal, it was no surprise to find Rick Fairless the recipient of the coveted Sweepstakes Award at the Grand National Roadster Show held in Oakland, California, in 2004.

The perfect chopper, in Fairless' eyes, is one that turns heads but can still be ridden hard on the roads. "Real choppers have to have originality and rideability. Unless a bike is functional, it doesn't matter how bad-assed it looks."

Frame: **Rigid**

Engine: **Evolution-type**

Date Photographed: **2004**

Frame: **Rigid**

Engine: **Evolution-type**

Date Photographed: **2004**

Frame: **Rigid**

Engine: **Evolution-type**

Date Photographed: **2004**

Chapter 11

Al Gaither

NEW KID, OLD BLOCK

Al Gaither of Wichita, Kansas' Chronic Choppers stands out among the new breed of chopper builders operating on the show and street circuits these days, thanks to his readily identifiable vision of what a chopper should be. At a time when cruiser motorcycles increasingly emerge from manufacturers' design rooms looking as innocuous and affable as minivans, Gaither's radically proportioned choppers are about as subtle and inviting as an AK-47. His chassis, welded together one at a time in custom-engineered jigs, are identified by their impossibly tall backbone stretch and lazy rakes of 42 degrees and longer. His handlebars are often lengths of massive chain links welded together and placed in risers topped with menacing-looking piked endcaps. A Chronic chopper is the sort of motorcycle that captures the original outlaw chopper essence, a machine that tells the world to step off in no uncertain terms.

Gaither, a youngster still in his 30s, prefers choppers that will get a rider noticed both for their style and their performance. His favorite engine for powering Chronic's rides is a whopping 124-cubic-inch Evolution-style stroker from S&S Cycle. Even though a Chronic chopper may measure a good 10 feet from tire to tire and ride on forks 10 inches and longer than stock, they're meant to go and show; nitrous oxide systems aren't uncommon, and the big-inch motors typically breathe through large-velocity S&S carburetors with Chronic's curvy, open-ended drag pipes announcing their presence to the world. With a four-man staff of technicians, mechanics, and painters, Chronic, over the last five years, has developed a shop where customers can have their dream bike built by a crew intimately involved with the process; custom paint, sheetmetal pattern cutting and fitting, and even machine-shop work is all performed in-house. The results are motorcycles that resemble something Van Helsing would ride on his way to kick the Terminator's ass.

"We aren't trying to build choppers that everybody's going to like or bikes that you can buy little toys of down at the local Toys-R-Us," one of Chronic's staffers said with refreshing frankness. "Choppers are supposed to be bad-ass and that's what we provide."

Frame: **Rigid**

Engine: **Evolution-type**

Date Photographed: **2002**

Frame: **Softail-type**

Engine: **Twin cam**

Date Photographed: **2001**

Frame: **Rigid**

Engine: **Evolution-type**

Date Photographed: **2001**

Chapter 12
Kendall Johnson
THE MAD CLOWN

The name "Kendall Johnson" is about the biggest thing to grace this lush hill country around Winston Salem, North Carolina, since tobacco.

With a riding season that keeps the roar of motorcycles filling the valleys and hillsides nearly year-round, Johnson launched his business in nearby Germantown in the early 1980s, specializing in high-performance engine work for Harley-Davidsons. In time, his work at culling near-unheard-of levels of horsepower from Milwaukee's venerable pushrod V-Twin was getting the Johnson name recognized in national magazines and by chopper builders who were placing his powerplants in their machines.

With his own mental notebook overflowing with ideas, Johnson launched Kendall Johnson Customs (KJC) in 1992 and today works with his long-time staff building 12 to 15 full-blown custom choppers and cruisers each year. KJC will build any style of American-made motorcycle customers desire, from a quick-throttled, Pro-Street stroker to a bagger that eats up the attention as voraciously as it eats up the miles. KJC's expertise with an airbrush has established Johnson's Killer Clown choppers among the industry's most memorable and outrageous custom motorcycles.

Looking like a cross between a scene from a concert by gangsta rappers Insane Clown Posse and a Felliniesque circus nightmare, Johnson's paint schemes grab a viewer's attention and hold it rapt for hours. Viewers pore over each of the intricate scenarios and tribal images buried within the elaborate paint.

In recent years, Johnson, who operates his shop along with his wife, Missy, has started to engender some fairly high-profile notoriety for his works, having been commissioned to create choppers for the Camel Roadhouse custom builders showcase. His 2003 Camel bike later made its way into the pages of *Easyriders* magazine and then on to a cross-country tour of New Zealand that was broadcast on cable's Speed Channel.

Johnson can proudly say that his custom motorcycles haven't changed much in the past two decades. They're still built around his otherworldly paint skills and feature engines capable of blowing the doors off just about anything they encounter on the roads. A winning formula if ever there was one.

Frame: **Softail-type**

Engine: **Evolution-type**

Date Photographed: **2003**

Frame: **Rigid**

Engine: **Evolution-type**

Date Photographed: **2003**

Frame: **Softail-type**

Engine: **Evolution-type**

Date Photographed: **2004**

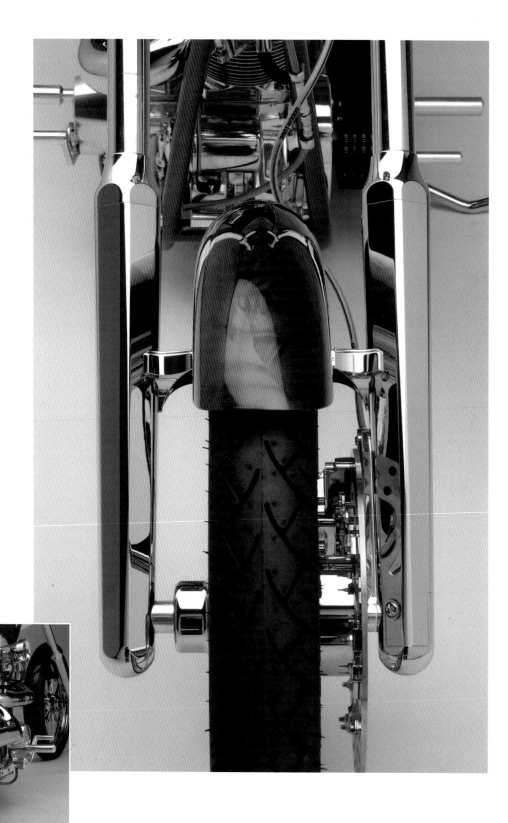

Chapter 13
Billy Lane
THE LADIES' MAN

Some chopper builders will tell you that the hardest part of their job is the nuts-and-bolts aspect of building one-of-a-kind motorcycles. Fabricating motorcycle parts from raw metal, bolting and welding them into a cohesive shape and structure, and making them function, sometimes better than stock parts, is all part of the allure and challenge of being a master motorcycle craftsman—but for Billy Lane, there's more to it than that.

Lane, of Melbourne, Florida, has, at the age of 34, pretty much sussed what it is that people find so sexy, so alluring, and so unforgettable about choppers. Lane has won almost every episode of the Discovery Channel's popular *Biker Build-Off* series he's appeared on, his outrageous chopper designs consistently winning crowd approval over the formidable works of top builders.

It's the same at custom motorcycle shows and in the pages of enthusiast magazines, places where Billy Lane's bikes are instantly recognizable for their odd combination of the brashly innovative and the familiar. Control knobs and fuel petcocks are frequently made from early twentieth-century plumbing fixtures. Old Ford truck grilles find their way onto fuel tanks. Lane's hand-crafted exhaust systems coil their way under and through his machines' drivetrains and engines and exit out the rear fender. His gas tanks are lovingly adorned with portraits of vintage pin-up girls that wouldn't look out of place on the nose of a World War II fighter plane.

But Lane's mechanical expression seldom stops with just a nostalgia trip; the hubless rear wheel on his infamous PsychoBilly Cadillac was built during a nerve-shattering three-month run leading up to the annual Daytona Beach Bike Week celebration, utilizing technology from high-tech helicopters.

Lane says his visual cues can come from nearly any source, be it the natural curves of a woman's body or from his extensive personal archive of classic chopper photos and biker artifacts. The results are choppers that have kept the crowds gawking and the competition constantly rushing back to their sketchbooks for inspiration.

Frame: **Rigid**

Engine: **Knucklehead**

Date Photographed: **2003**

Frame: **Rigid**

Engine: **Shovelhead**

Date Photographed: **2003**

Frame: **Rigid**

Engine: **Panhead**

Date Photographed: **2004**

Chapter 14

Donny Loos & Jeff Cochran

THE TRADITIONAL CHOPPER LIVES ON

At 45 years of age, Donny Loos of Miamitown, Ohio, is too young to be nostalgic about the days of D.A. haircuts, Elvis (when he was still skinny), and raw-edged early-style choppers. You wouldn't know that after taking a ride with Loos and company, who are making quite a splash on the chopper set with the rigidly traditional rigid-frame bikes rolling out of the oddly named Sucker Punch Sally shop.

Loos and business partner Jeff Cochran both come from families with rich custom motorcycle backgrounds, with the Cochran clan's love of rending and riding the big metal going back three generations. Loos' love of classic customs extends to a collection of hot rod cars, including a 1937 Ford coupe and a 1934 Ford convertible, both of which he says contain that certain greasy magic that characterizes S.P.S. choppers.

"I remember seeing classic choppers as a kid, and I thought they were so cool. I've been through all the other custom chopper stuff from fatbikes to wild stuff like a big tire stretch chopper I built a few years ago. But out on one of our classic choppers, they're so much easier to ride and they handle so much better that you can actually stop and turn around in a single lane," Loos said with a laugh.

The typical S.P.S. chopper owes more to the machines that emerged from backyard garages in the late 1950s and early 1960s than to any of the latter-day custom choppers characterized by one-off sheetmetal parts and high-concept designs. Nearly all the parts are off-the-shelf items, with an emphasis on old-school bits like metalflake vinyl seats, rebuilt vintage Shovelhead or Knucklehead engines, white rubber handgrips, and tall apehanger handlebars that are uncluttered by so much as a brake lever or clutch cable. Instead, Loos favors the foot-clutch/jockey shift combination and a strong rear disc brake for stopping.

By bolting together rather than fabricating all their bikes, S.P.S. can produce machines that even youthful chopper enthusiasts can afford (they list for about $14,000) and can be completed, from the ground up, in about three weeks. Production has run at a dizzying 30 bikes for each of the two years S.P.S. has been in business, and the elegant, antique-looking choppers have graced the pages of magazines both in the United States and Europe. "Our customers are younger guys and guys who appreciate old-school hot rods. We may not fabricate everything ourselves, but we express ourselves through paint and detail, and people love it," Loos said.

Frame: **Rigid**

Engine: **Knucklehead**

Date Photographed: **2004**

Frame: **Rigid**

Engine: **Knucklehead**

Date Photographed: **2002**

Frame: **Rigid**

Engine: **Panhead**

Date Photographed: **1999**

Chapter 15
Michael Pugliese
FOR THE LOVE OF IT

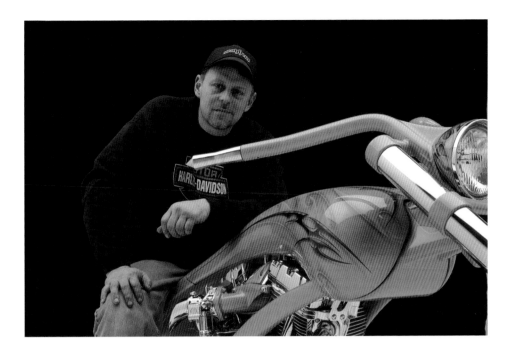

Mike Pugliese is a rare bird among today's chopper artists. During the decade this native New Yorker has been applying welding torch to metal, Pugliese says he hasn't really sold many of the bikes he's built.

"I do this because I love it," he said with a sly laugh. "Otherwise, I'd be crazy to stay up all night working on these things for anybody else." A home-building contractor by trade, Pugliese is one of those massively talented craftsmen who creates award-winning custom motorcycles simply because it's in his soul. "The money really doesn't mean anything," he asserts. "I build cool stuff for my friends because it makes me happy to see how much they like it."

Pugliese's friends must be a very happy bunch—one of his choppers rolled away with the coveted Best in Show award at the annual Rat's Hole Custom Show held during Daytona Beach Bike Week in 2004, competing against the most talented motorcycle craftsmen from around the world.

Pugliese began fiddling with motorcycles in the early 1990s, after purchasing a bone-stock Harley-Davidson Fatboy and realizing "it looked just like everybody else's bike." The gas tanks were soon stretched with some homemade sheetmetal panels and molded in thanks to bodyshop skills Mike had picked up at a local fender-repair garage as a teen. The rear swingarm was widened, and Pugliese mounted a wider rear tire.

Pugliese says the chopper bug has yet to loosen its grip on his psyche. At 43, he says the level of competition between builders has reached a fevered state. "What looked outstanding last year might not even get anybody's attention this year. It's at an insane level, like going from a horse and buggy to a Dodge Viper in a couple of years," he jokes.

Maintaining his place at the summit of builders is simply a matter of following some of the early rules that Mike used to launch his career a decade ago. He still sketches out the blueprints for his custom bikes on huge, life-sized sheets of illustration board. He still uses long forks, roadworthy engines, and minimal bodywork as mainstays—that, and a love of tinkering. "I just can't leave anything alone once I've started working on it. Do that long enough, and you end up with a great chopper."

Frame: **Softail-type**

Engine: **Evolution-type**

Date Photographed: **1999**

Frame: **Softail-type**

Engine: **Twincam**

Date Photographed: **2002**

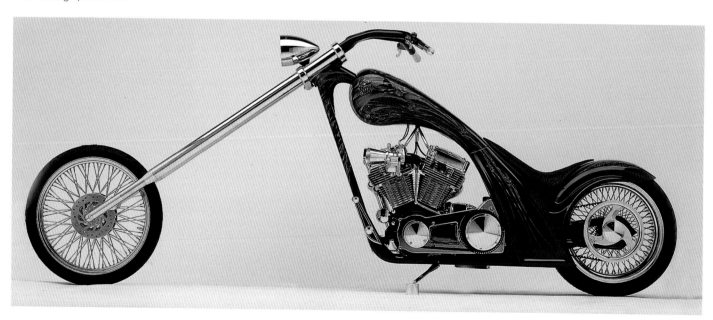

Frame: **Softail-type**

Engine: **Twin cam**

Date Photographed: **2004**

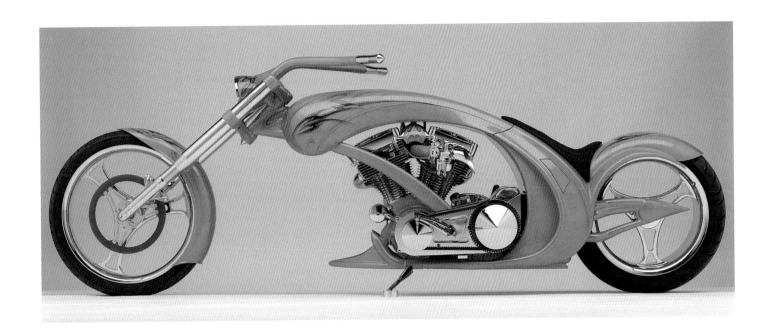

Chapter 16

Kim Suter

KANSAS CITY STYLE

Kansas City's Kim Suter, owner and CEO of KC Creations, one of the Midwest's biggest and best-known custom motorcycle emporiums, loves to be challenged by the choppers and custom Hogs he assembles. Suter's usual choppers are laid-back longbikes with high handlebars and lush paint schemes.

Though Suter is normally a very quiet guy, he's also a big guy you wouldn't want to mess with. The man obviously spends some time in the gym. The big pipes find their way onto his bikes, too; Suter uses a "Big Inch" muscle logo on all of his work.

Suter, who has been a motorcyclist since he was a kid, got into motorcycle customization when he rode his Softail to Sturgis in 1986 and realized it looked like every other Softail at Sturgis that year. He tore into the bike, things got a little out of hand, and by 1995 he had quit his job as a vice president and general manager of a gasoline business to start KC Creations.

KC Creations was also an *Easyriders* store until recently, when the *Easyriders* store program ended. KC Creations is now a branded Big Dog dealership, and Suter sells Big Dog motorcycles alongside his hand-crafted two-wheeled masterpieces.

Suter's elaborate customs have gained him a membership in the Hamsters motorcycle club, making him one of the elite members of that group who has earned his way into the club as a builder rather than simply as a well-heeled customer.

Suter's shop is a family business. His wife Cheryl works the same number of hours each day as he does, handling much of the administrative side of the business. She must be doing a spectacular job because KC Creations was recently honored as one of Kansas City's 25 most outstanding small businesses by the *Kansas City Small Business Monthly*. It's a safe bet that when Suter first got a wild hair to customize his Harley nearly twenty years ago, he never dreamed it would lead to such an honor.

Frame: **Softail-type**

Engine: **Evolution-type**

Date Photographed: **2003**

Frame: **Softail-type**

Engine: **Evolution-type**

Date Photographed: **2002**

Frame: **Softail-type**

Engine: **Evolution-type**

Date Photographed: **2003**

Chapter 17

Russ Tom

IN HIS BLOOD

At a glance, Russ Tom's choppers bear little resemblance to the kinds of Harley-Davidson–based creations that his father, Carmen, made at their family's Seattle dealership. Carmen Tom was a World War II navy veteran who returned home from the war at the perfect time to launch himself into the country's growing motorcycle subculture. After selling imported machines and racing Honda dirtbikes with Russ and the three other Tom sons, Carmen, always the clever entrepreneur, began designing, building, and selling chopper conversion kits for at-home builders in the 1960s. The kits and their signature coffin-style gas tanks sold faster than you could say king-and-queen seat, and by the 1980s the Tom name was synonymous with custom motorcycling in the Pacific Northwest.

Young Russell Tom took over the family business, Downtown Harley-Davidson, in 1997 and never lost his love for performance bikes like the early Hondas and Maico off-roaders and the custom choppers his father helped introduce to the region. This goes a long way toward understanding the iconoclastic vision behind Russ Tom's café racer Big Twin, a wild ride combining the thick, all-aluminum alloy perimeter frame from a late-model sportbike with the thundering power of an American-made V-Twin engine.

Tom's version of the quintessential street racer has all the bells and whistles you'd expect to find on a 190-horsepower Suzuki GSX-R or a svelte Ducati superbike, but in this instance, the lightweight, single-sided swingarm is hand-built from Tom's own designs, while the flat-topped gas tank and low-profile handlebars are low enough to allow maximum airflow over the machine at speed.

Tom got his start customizing an old Honda CB 750 Four in an elaborately painted and molded rigid frame, and he's never lost his appreciation for changing the lines of a motorcycle through the use of handmade exotic bodywork and sheetmetal molding. A black Evolution-powered custom he built in 2003 is enveloped in a breathtaking array of flowing, angular bodywork, its massive collector exhaust poking through the lower fairing like a smokestack; his innovative Harley customs are both traditional and groundbreaking, combining the best parts of custom motorcycling's past, present, and future, just like Russell Tom himself.

Frame: **Swingarm-type**

Engine: **Twin cam**

Date Photographed: **2002**

Frame: **Rigid**

Engine: **Evolution-type**

Date Photographed: **1997**

Frame: **Softail-type**

Engine: **Evolution-type**

Date Photographed: **2000**

Chapter 18

Mark Warrick

SPEED AND CUSTOM

Mark Warrick likes to sweat the details when it comes to building choppers. In fact, the small nuts and bolts and the hand-fabricated accessories that riders can't buy over the counter at their local Harley parts emporium are precisely what Warrick's Amarillo, Texas, shop, Soncy Road Speed and Custom, specializes in. The 35-year-old started the business some 15 years ago having mastered the art of refurbishing vintage American hot rod cars. The chopper business, Warrick said, presents builders with quite a different set of challenges and skills tests than do custom cars, due to the constant and relentless competition between chopper builders. Oh, yeah—customers can be pretty tough to please too.

Thankfully, a background in chopper parts fabrication for the likes of Paul Yaffe and Jim Nasi Customs has helped Warrick gain the approval of his peers and customers, plus a few magazine editors who've placed his creations on their covers several times in recent years.

"I'm the kind of guy who just can't leave anything alone without tinkering with it, so I've always been a kind of behind-the-scenes guy, somebody who works for months on something like an axle cover or an oil tank before putting it on a completed bike," Warrick said. "There's too many choppers being built by guys who don't pay attention to the small stuff, and that's what our strength is and what makes our bikes really stand out from the norm."

Because Warrick's crew would rather fabricate their parts than simply pull them from a dealer's shelf, they only complete about five bikes each year. One of their choppers can take up to eight months to complete and cost as much as $50,000. But what a rider gets for that money is a machine embodying the build-it, don't-buy-it ethos that's so important to new-generation builders. Warrick's exhaust pipes are always one-off designs that are never repeated on another motorcycle, and he's unique in applying nickel plating rather than chrome to hard parts.

Meanwhile, Warrick's ghost flame paint is said to be of industry-leading quality. And if you're waiting for one of his rare choppers, keep one thing in mind: "Customers have to let me alone to work, because once I have a general idea of what they want, I'll take it from there. Too much input means they usually want a bike that looks like something they've seen somewhere else, and that's not what we do."

Frame: **Rigid**

Engine: **Evolution-type**

Date Photographed: **2003**

Frame: **Softail-type**

Engine: **Evolution-type**

Date Photographed: **2003**

Frame: **Rigid**

Engine: **Panhead**

Date Photographed: **2003**

Chapter 19

Paul Yaffe

EXCELLENCE PERSONIFIED

With a grand prize in the prestigious Oakland Grand National Roadster Show to his credit, showing up as the subject of more magazine articles than J. Lo's rear end, and a client list that sent every custom chopper he built rolling out of his Scottsdale, Arizona, workshop for a very handsome price, there should be no doubt that Paul Yaffe has arrived. But even the boyish, soft-spoken master mechanic couldn't have been prepared for what happened after appearing on the Discovery Channel's Biker Build-Off series in the winter of 2004.

"Every bike, every prototype project, every rolling chassis, everything in the shop was sold," he told Easyriders magazine, astonished at his own success. But there's no reason Yaffe should be taken aback by the admiration his machines have engendered among chopper riders, everyday bikers, and plain old folks who've never thrown a leg across a motorcycle seat. Paul Yaffe Originals, the name he's splashed on his shop and ever-growing parts line, has always forged its own path in the custom motorcycle scene, presenting high-end accessories and complete motorcycles with all the engineering know-how of an Apache helicopter and all the style of a Lamborghini.

He was among the first builders to experiment with heretofore untried concepts like two-level gas tanks with radically stretched contours, pro street frames with backbones curved to accept his tanks, rear fenders such as the unit mounted to his silver masterpiece "Double Trouble III," which attached directly to the Softail frame to replicate the looks of a rigid, and innovative exhaust pipes that could wake a slumbering grizzly bear from hibernation. His roster of designs includes both pro street lowriders and some of the spiciest stretch choppers ever to turn an axle, though all Yaffe machines share a graceful, almost art deco motif, full of flowing curves and jutting metalwork that wouldn't look out of place in Frank Lloyd Wright's sketchbook. While the Yaffe parts empire is currently among the largest in the entire aftermarket industry, Paul Yaffe still busies himself building motorcycles in the arid deserts of Arizona, in a self-driven quest to somehow outdo himself. He probably will.

Frame: **Swingarm-type**

Engine: **Evolution-type**

Date Photographed: **2000**

Frame: **Softail-type**

Engine: **Evolution-type**

Date Photographed: **2000**

Frame: **Softail-type**

Engine: **Evolution-type**

Date Photographed: **2003**

NEW BLOOD

Determining the future direction of choppers and custom motorcycles will take more than a crystal ball and a steady eye on the aftermarket industry. Few insiders could have (or did) predict that in the opening stages of the twenty-first century, choppers would be more popular than they were in what was considered the custom motorcycle's heyday in the 1960s and early 1970s.

The machines being produced by the current crop of builders also show us how difficult it is to predict where the chopper game is heading. Purveyors of traditional, bare-bones bobbers wrapped in simple black primer and wire wheels have found audiences as have the high-end technicians who can rend expensive, aircraft-quality billet aluminum into sleek, otherworldly designs that still represent the essence of a chopper.

Undoubtedly overexposure will threaten the chopper's popularity, but despite the huge number of TV programs, magazine articles, and books that chronicle this popular folk-art form, the truth cannot be ignored that choppers, for the average motorcyclist, are still something of a novelty. At any motorcycle rally, T-shirts advertising this or that chopper shop with iron-cross logos are everywhere, but actual choppers appear thin on the ground. In some countries, choppers have already taken a back seat to the Streetfighter, a radically customized, high-performance superbike that borrows the chopper's baroque attention to detail, but can be built on the average rider's budget (and often from wrecked or disassembled motorcycles). And for every popular movement, there comes an inevitable backlash, something choppers have managed to avoid despite nearly five years of unprecedented time in the spotlight.

The fact that choppers remain time-intensive, mostly hand-built pieces of rolling sculpture presents specific challenges to the latest entrants into the custom motorcycle game: should they focus their energies on making choppers as affordable and accessible as the kit bike builders did in the 1970s at the risk of sacrificing quality and originality of vision, or do they risk alienating younger, less affluent motorcyclists by staying true to their unique visions of mechanical perfection and exclusivity?

For some of the builders who represent the notable new blood of the chopper movement, both of these concerns have been addressed. Some have decided to focus on further elevating choppers to unheard-of pinnacles of technological and artful invention, creating motorcycles so far advanced in aesthetics it may take decades for the public's eye to catch up with them. Still others are embracing the recent past by attempting to make choppers an everyman's motorcycle while still offering a departure from the tedium of bolt-on custom motorcycles.

There may never be another time when motorcycles—or any vehicles—built and designed with a singular vision so capture the public's imagination. But the new blood convinces us that choppers, in whatever incarnation, will always be with us.

Chapter 20

Roger Goldammer

CANADIAN CLASS

There's a rich vein among chopper purists who contend that anything hinting of the high-tech and the expensive belongs nowhere near a chopper. These self-anointed keepers of the hardtail faith congregate in Internet chat rooms and in the letters pages of custom motorcycle–enthusiast magazines to heap dis and envy on builders who aren't afraid to move the art of the custom motorcycle into the twenty-first century. The twenty-first century is a place where Canadian chopper builder Roger Goldammer is quite comfortable, as his G-Force line of parts and complete, ground-up motorcycles, have attained the admiration of metallurgists, mechanical engineers, and open-minded chopper fanatics from around the world.

Goldammer Cycle Works opened its doors in 1997 and quickly focused its energies on taking the owner's promise to bring advanced quality to the chopper game to the streets. While most of today's chopper parts are constructed of a quality far surpassing that of custom parts from just 20 years ago, Goldammer went a step further than chromoly steel and TIG welding with his single-sided swingarm, air-lift chassis. Like a prop from a *Star Wars* serial, the frame is infused with a science class full of gee-whiz details; constructed of 1 1/4-inch mild steel DOM tubing, the cross-members are made from billet aluminum for extra strength while the rear ends are built to accept Goldammer's own billet swingarm, machined from a solid, 170-pound block of the durable alloy.

The eccentrically mounted hub almost appears to float above the road, while pavement imperfections are smoothed out via an air-lift suspension system fed by a tiny compressor hidden within the chassis itself. Goldammer has invested similar in-depth research into the radically smooth, one-piece billet front ends he attaches to the six or seven choppers his shop churns out each year, ensuring these machines ride as smoothly as they look.

While all of this mechanical wizardry may run the risk of rendering a chopper less elegant and minimal than traditionalists would prefer, Goldammer's low-riding chops are every bit as stripped down and spare in appearance as a digger Sportster, circa 1972. No need to fear the future, Roger Goldammer's designs assure us, not when they can keep choppers looking this cool and riding this strong.

Frame: **Softail-type**

Engine: **Twin cam**

Date Photographed: **2004**

Frame: **Softail-type**

Engine: **Special construction alternator/generator evolution-type**

Date Photographed: **2004**

Chapter 21

Jesse Jurrens

LEGEND IN HIS OWN TIME

Jesse Jurrens' choppers are perhaps not as well known as, say, the upscale custom bikes created by Paul Yaffe or the block-long telescopic forks popularized by Sweden's Tolle Denisch, but they are no less revolutionary. Jurrens, the owner and CEO of Legends Air Ride Suspension, makes his presence known every time a softail-chopper rider rides his machine over a bump or through a pothole . . . as the inventor of the air-ride suspension system.

Jurrens, a youthful thirty-something, has made the business of riding choppers a lot more tolerable for tens of thousands of bikers the world over. Today's high-end choppers, which easily cost as much as luxury cars or sport utility vehicles, tend to be used by older riders who have little patience—or lumbar support—for the rough ride provided by rigid frames and unforgiving highways. Jurrens' suspension units, which operate on an adjustable-density layer of compressed air, have permitted chopped motorcycles to become more than just exotic vehicles to be admired as art. With a more comfortable ride, they're serious road machines, capable of racking up long miles just like their stock counterparts.

When Jurrens isn't busy making the job of riding choppers more tolerable, he's busy designing his own rides at Independent Cycle Inc. (I.C.I.), his custom chopper–building firm launched in Rapid City, South Dakota. The engineering acumen necessary to produce air-assisted suspension systems has served the lanky and slightly foreboding Jurrens well when it comes to designing chopper chassis. His Low Life frame maintains one of the lowest seat heights in the industry and is renowned for its roadworthiness and fluid, flowing lines. Likewise, the sheetmetal work that characterizes an Independent Cycle chopper is an exercise in metallic motion.

The editors of Hot Bike magazine once described a chopper that Jurrens built as being comprised of "sleek lines that seem to neither begin nor end," while the recent addition of wheels, handlebars, and fenders to the I.C.I. line has only helped galvanize this unique chopper builder's vision among the competition.

Frame: **Softail-type**

Engine: **Evolution-type**

Date Photographed: **2004**

Frame: **Softail-type**

Engine: **Evolution-type**

Date Photographed: **2004**

Chapter 22

Brian Klock

DEDICATION AND DRIVE

When South Dakota's Brian Klock launched his initial venture into the custom motorcycle game, saying he did so on a shoestring budget would be a classic understatement. The former journalism and photography major had, at his estimate, maybe $4,000 to spend on parts and a tiny, 700-square-foot garage for a shop. But Klock trusted his eye for design and his love of choppers, both of which he'd developed while studying photography and custom motorcycle magazines.

His affinity for the heroes of the chopper world brought Klock, of Mitchell, South Dakota, some of his first national recognition. A digger-style chopper that Massachusetts' Dave Perewitz had built back in 1979 inspired Klock, 37, to customize a late-model Harley-Davidson Sportster into an updated replica of the Perewitz bike named after the Eagles' song "One Of These Nights."

And instead of simply emulating 1970s-style customs, his shop, Klock Werks, created an entire rubber-mounted chassis to house a late-model Evolution Sportster engine, hand-fabricated oil and gas tanks, plus a set of stunning wrap-around open exhaust pipes that exit the machine from just under the oil bag. Though the Klock Werks crew has built choppers in a variety of configurations, they're among the few firms focusing their skills on making the oft-ignored Harley-Davidson Sportster a popular choice for chopper builders.

"We're in a town of 15,000 people and I always tell guys who work at the shop that they'd better learn to appreciate every kind of bike on the road, from baggers to Sportsters and Buells and choppers," said Klock, who now rolls in the rarified air of the chopper-building heroes of his childhood. "And because I started off with so little money, if a guy walks into the shop with just a few grand to spend, I'm gonna spend that money like it's my own, making sure his bike comes out with some really cool, really unique theme no matter how much money he has to spend."

Since getting started in 1997, Brian Klock and partner Dan Cheesman have experienced a fairly rapid ride to recognition for their firm's ecumenical approach to chopper building. Klock never forgets to note that he wouldn't be appearing on TV shows and in the pages of magazines like *IronWorks* and *American Iron* if he hadn't received some very helpful guidance from established chopper customizers he'd met along the way.

"I bought an old Police Harley FXRS in 1992 and tore it apart," Klock said, "and when I went to the Hollister Rally with [custom motorcycle seat maker] Danny Gray, I met people like Jesse James and saw his shop and I met Donnie Smith who was totally cool. I didn't know rake dimensions from a hole in the ground, but he was willing to talk with me and trade ideas. I was blown away by how cool these guys were."

While his career trajectory seems clearly headed skyward, Klock feels that chopper building has no rules; they just need to be crazy. Klock says he still thrills to the look of satisfaction on the faces of his customers when they roll into a crowd of bikes on one of the choppers Klock Werks has built. "When a customer pulls up at a poker run and everyone knows that's his own bike and the smile the owner gets, that's what makes it all worthwhile."

Frame: **Swingarm-type**

Engine: **Sportster**

Date Photographed: **2002**

Frame: **Softail-type**

Engine: **Evolution-type**

Date Photographed: **2002**

Chapter 23
Tom Langton
MAKING A RUMBLE

In an age of forced nostalgia and cookie-cutter custom bikes, Tom Langton proves there's no path better than the one previously unexplored. His portfolio of custom motorcycles owes as much to the twenty-first century as it does to the twentieth, with exotic carbon fiber, lightweight aluminum, and tricks from the world of high-speed motorcycle road racing all working their way into this young Canadian's machines.

In 2003, for instance, Langton was commissioned by Camel to build a custom bike for their annual Camel Roadhouse promotion. The 26-year-old produced a mad, over-the-top Harley-Davidson–powered café racer that looked like a cross between an AMA Superbike and one of Eric Buell's wet dreams.

Not limited by influences, fashion, or what the other guy is building, Langton shocked the competition—and earned himself *Easyriders* magazine's Builder of The Year Award for 2003—by busting out only a few months later with a classically styled early chopper that looked like something a World War II vet might have raced on one of California's dry lake beds in the late 1940s. His sleek and very thoroughly engineered El Camino chopper—with its lush gold finish, Cannondale mountain-bike brakes, and handmade oil tank mounted cleverly inside the rear fender—was a tribute to early car customizers like Ed Roth who Langton says provided a major influence for his work.

"I guess you could say my signature style is that I don't really have a signature bike," said Langton, whose love affair with all things two-wheeled has been with him since childhood. The Delta, Ontario, homeboy is known to take his time crafting the two ground-up choppers he completes each year, meticulously engineering every component from wheel design to sheetmetal and forks.

"That's what it takes to design something that can truly be said to be handmade," he says. Langton is proud of his keen eye for motorcycling exotica, borrowing elements from machines as diverse as a Ducati 999 and Kawasaki's pavement-ripping ZX-10 Ninja. Not exactly what the old guard would consider proper chopping fodder, but the fiercely independent Langton says the main rule with choppers is to create something controversial.

"I always try to be original, and you have to try and be provocative, especially when so many people are building choppers right now," he said. "But whatever style it is, whether it's a café racer or a traditional, long chopper, what they all have in common is two wheels and an engine and you have to straddle it. And if you can't take those basic design elements and make them provocative, you're not making good art."

Frame: **Rigid**

Engine: **Shovelhead**

Date Photographed: **2003**

Frame: **Rigid**

Engine: **Evolution-type**

Date Photographed: **2003**

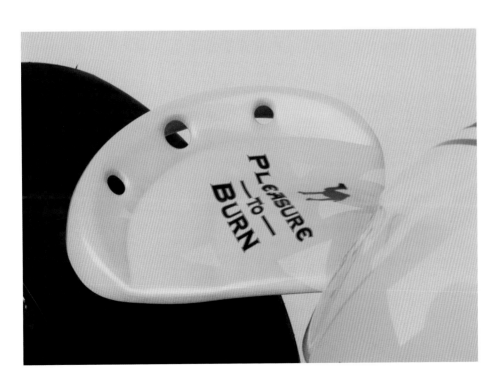

Chapter 24

Kai Morrison & Jason Kangas

NEW LOOKS, OLD COOL

The tale of how Kai Morrison and Jason Kangas got their start in the chopper trade sounds like one of the old Western tales the pair grew up hearing in their hometown of Sioux Falls, South Dakota. They attended school together since the second grade and studied machine shop at the same technical school, but both men had decided to open small businesses customizing motorcycles unbeknownst to the other.

In time, the pair realized they were sharing not only customers, but a raw-edged vision of what a modern chopper should look like. The decision to join forces, at Twisted Choppers, seemed like the logical thing to do, Morrison said. With the steady clangor of metalworking ringing in the background, Morrison explained how, at an age when most of his riding buddies were still popping freeway wheelies on their sportbikes, he's become one of the respected young guns of the chopper set.

"I don't really know what got us into choppers," "Morrison said. "I guess we both liked custom hot rods and after I came across an old Sportster, I was never satisfied with the way it looked, so I kept cutting and welding and raking and changing stuff until we were happy."

That was in 2000, and since then Twisted Choppers' hard-edged sheetmetal parts, flat-black finishes, skate-rat attitudes, and postmodern take on the chopper has put a youthful face on what's often considered an older man's game.

Morrison readily acknowledges that not every biker quite knows what to make of his shop's, well, twisted creations. "We're still way ahead of what the norm is out here and sometimes I catch people staring at our bikes like they don't quite know what they're looking at. But it seems like they're catching on to us, because we have customers bringing in their bikes and they want the same kinds of changes we've been putting on our choppers."

With an eye for wickedly mean-looking choppers, Kai's rigid Shovelhead has a Friscoed 3.5-gallon Sportster tank with a piked cap and a 21-inch front wheel with no fender or brake, and he swears by the more-affordable vintage Harley-Davidson powerplants from the 1940s through the 1960s. "I'll admit it. I like the harder-edged lines, not the really smooth stuff. I like an aggressive-looking chopper and live by the less-is-definitely-more ethos," said Morrison who, refreshingly, admits that rat bikes, primer-as-paint, and the odd bits of rust don't really turn him off.

Today, Twisted Choppers turns out something near 15 full customs each year while still performing custom work on hundreds of local rides. And it doesn't cost an arm and a leg, either. "It's a lot cheaper living here than on either coast, so a bike that'll cost $60,000 in L.A. will only set you back half that here," he said.

Frame: **Rigid**

Engine: **Panhead**

Date Photographed: **2002**

Frame: **Softail-type**

Engine: **Evolution-type**

Date Photographed: **2003**

Chapter 25
Hank Young
HOT ROD HEART

When Hank Young splashed onto the national chopper-building scene in 2003 with his eye-popping Flying Pan chopper, it was as if the past and the present had collided in one incredible custom motorcycle. The svelte, almost Spartan chopper had the narrow midsection of an old board track racer from the 1920s, and the front leaf-spring forks looked like something from an Indian Motorcycle Company parts catalog, circa 1933.

But Young, who made his bones in the custom car business with his Ford Street Hot Rod Parts out of Marietta, Georgia, was on more than a nostalgia trip; the Flying Pan was powered by a fully modern S&S motor (with retro Panhead valve covers, naturally) had a handmade modern chassis, and ran on low-profile radial tires. Most of the rest of the machine was an exercise in resourcefulness—like the huge, finned rear brake culled from a 1950s Buick—and ingenuity, demonstrated by the front chassis downtube built from an old car axle.

"I've always loved the lean, swoopy look of those old board track racers and hot rods so I guess this just came naturally," Young says. He entered the chopper trade at a time when the cost of producing ground-up custom cars was becoming prohibitively expensive, and so he saw motorcycles as a much-needed outlet for his burgeoning creativity. For Young, who has built dozens of classic cars over the years, the chopper world proved to be a perfect place to meld his two favorite mechanical disciplines.

Since the launch of the Flying Pan, Hank Young's melding of classic custom cars and choppers has earned him a following that the hot rod trade could only have hinted at. One of his machines, a funky, 1940s-style Knucklehead bobber, was selected for a slot in the "Art of the Chopper" exhibit at Rapid City, South Dakota's Journey Museum in 2003, alongside machines from the likes of Arlen Ness and Billy Lane.

Like a prop from Marlon Brando's *The Wild One*, the bobber bike came replete with stealthy, black-spoked wheels and a rough-hewn leather saddle. Though Young says he thoroughly enjoys fabricating parts for his retro choppers and bobbers, he's proven resourceful in using everything from the Internet to international contacts to track down the rare NOS parts that appeal to his purist customers. Rumor has it the Young compound is knee-deep in ancient parts stock, allowing the shop to build choppers using original Harley-Davidson XA springer forks, cloth-covered oil lines, tin primary covers, and single-sided drum brakes rather than substituting classic parts with modern replacements.

Young admits that choppers, while bursting with creativity and new ideas, haven't been as cheap to build as he initially expected. But perfection seldom comes cheap.

Frame: **Rigid**

Engine: **Panhead**

Date Photographed: **2003**

Frame: **Swingarm-type**

Engine: **Knucklehead**

Date Photographed: **2003**

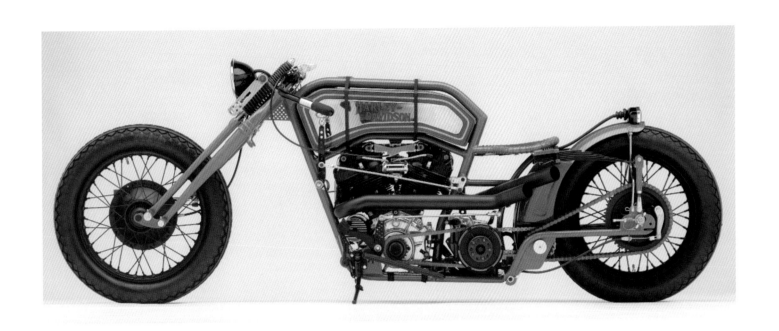

Index